JIMI HENDRIX

A Musician's Collection

The status of Jimi Hendrix as the definitive guitar player is well documented in other publications. This collection has been put together for ALL musicians attracted to Jimi's compositions. They are presented here in standard Piano/Vocal/Guitar format. It is an excellent source book that provides a unique perspective of his music.

Exclusively Distributed by
Hal Leonard Publishing Corporation
7777 West Bluemound Road P.O. Box 13819 Milwaukee, WI 53213

Color photography: ED CARAEFF
Photo research: BILL NITOPI

ISBN 0-7935-0419-8

AIN'T NO TELLING

Words and Music by
JIMI HENDRIX

Moderate rock

Well there ain't no,

ain't no, ain't no tell - in', ba - by, _____ when you will

see me a - gain. If I pray it will be to - mor - row. _____

Well, the sun - rise, sun - rise, is

BOLD AS LOVE

Words and Music by
JIMI HENDRIX

the Ax - is. ___ He knows ev - 'ry-thing. Yeah, ___ yeah. ___

Guitar solo - ad lib.

Play 6 times

ALL ALONG THE WATCHTOWER

Words and Music by
BOB DYLAN

There must be some kind a way

out - ta here, ___ said the jok - er to the thief. ___

BURNING OF THE MIDNIGHT LAMP

Words and Music by
JIMI HENDRIX

CAN YOU SEE ME

Words and Music by
JIMI HENDRIX

Can you hear _

CASTLES MADE OF SAND

Words and Music by
JIMI HENDRIX

Lyrics:

Down the street you can hear her scream, "You're a dis-grace," as she
In-di-an brave who be-fore he was ten played
was a young girl whose heart was a frown 'cause she

slams the door in his drunk-en face. And now he stands out-side and all the
war games in the woods with his In-di-an friends, and he built a dream that when he grew up he would
was crip-pled for life and she could-n't speak a sound. And she wished and prayed she could stop

neigh-bors start to gos-sip and drool.
be a fear-less war-ri-or In-di-an chief.
liv-in', so she de-ci-ded to die.

He
Man-y
She drew her

CROSSTOWN TRAFFIC

Words and Music by
JIMI HENDRIX

Repeat ad lib. and Fade

EZY RIDER

Words and Music by
JIMI HENDRIX

FIRE

By JIMI HENDRIX

FOXEY LADY

Words and Music by
JIMI HENDRIX

Fox - ey. Now - a, I see you___ come down on the scene,___

oh, fox - ey, You make me___ wan - na

get up and a scream. Fox - ey, oh ba-by, lis-ten now.

I've made up my mind,___ I'm tired of wast-ing all my

Em

Ooh, fox-ey la-dy, yeah, yeah._ You look so

good._ Fox-ey. Oh, yeah, fox-ey, fox-ey.

Yeah. Give us some, fox-ey. *You make me feel like a... very*

Repeat and Fade

fox-ey, fox-ey, Fox-ey.

GYPSY EYES

Words and Music by
JIMI HENDRIX

I love you gyp - sy eyes.

Well, al - right.

HAVE YOU EVER BEEN
(TO ELECTRIC LADYLAND)

Words and Music by
JIMI HENDRIX

HEY JOE

Words and Music by
BILLY ROBERTS

HOUSE BURNING DOWN

Words and Music by
JIMI HENDRIX

To Coda

Repeat ad lib. and Fade

IF SIX WAS NINE

Words and Music by
JIMI HENDRIX

KILLING FLOOR

Words and Music by
CHESTER BURNETT

LITTLE WING

Words and Music by
JIMI HENDRIX

LITTLE MISS LOVER

Words and Music by
JIMI HENDRIX

F7#9

Hey,   hey,   Lit - tle Miss Lov - er.   Well now a

so much   you and me   can dis - cov - er.   but I think we should start.

LOVE OR CONFUSION

Words and Music by
JIMI HENDRIX

Is that the stars _____ in the sky _____ or is

con - fu - sion?_____ Ma-ma, we must get to-geth-er ___ and

uh find out

ex - act - ly what we're tryin' to do.

Love __ or con - fu - sion?

LONG HOT SUMMER NIGHT

Words and Music by
JIMI HENDRIX

MANIC DEPRESSION

Words and Music by
JIMI HENDRIX

MAY THIS BE LOVE

Words and Music by
JIMI HENDRIX

So let them laugh, laugh_ at _ me.

So just as long _ as I have you to see me

through I have _ noth - ing to lose.

'Long_ as I _ have you.

PURPLE HAZE

Words and Music by
JIMI HENDRIX

RED HOUSE

Words and Music by
JIMI HENDRIX

REMEMBER

Words and Music by
JIMI HENDRIX

SPANISH CASTLE MAGIC

Words and Music by
JIMI HENDRIX

STONE FREE

By JIMI HENDRIX

UP FROM THE SKIES

Words and Music by
JIMI HENDRIX

If my dad-dy could see me now.

WAIT UNTIL TOMORROW

Words and Music by
JIMI HENDRIX

Well, I'm stand-ing here _ freez-ing in - side your gold-en gar-den.
Oh, Dol-ly Mae, _ how can you hang me up this way?
Owl Dol-ly Mae, girl, you must be in - sane, so un -

Uh, got my lad-der leaned up a - gainst your wall. To-
On the phone you said you want-ed to run off with me _ to-day. Now I'm
sure of your - self learn-ing from your un - sure win - dow pane.

Repeat and Fade

WILD THING

Words and Music by
CHIP TAYLOR

THE WIND CRIES MARY

Words and Music by
JIMI HENDRIX